Change Guidebook:
How to Sharpen Your Approach to Leading Organizational Change

By
Scot Holliday, Ed.D.

Table of Contents

List of Figures

List of Tables

Acknowledgements

Thank you to following people for reviewing this book and providing anecdotes:

- Jeff Austin, Senior Vice President - Internal Sustainability Manager at Wells Fargo
- Clyde V. Croswell, President, Community-L, Inc.; Professor, George Washington University; retired Lieutenant Colonel, U.S. Marines
- Ann Holliday, Journalist, Household Director
- Chad O. Holliday, Managing Director East Meets West Solutions LLC, former CEO and Chairman of DuPont
- Metri Holliday, Compensation Consultant, Discovery Communications
- Valerie Patrick, Senior Sustainability Coordinator, Bayer; Board Chair, Association for Climate Change Officers (ACCO)
- Paul Tebo, former V.P., Environment, Health and Safety, DuPont

Gratitude to Jon Fukuda, Co-Founder/ Principal of Limina Application Office for designing the book cover and selecting the book font.

Thank you to John Englander, Author/ Expert on Rising Sea Level; Chad H. Holliday, Graphic Artist; and Dan Kreeger, Executive Director, ACCO; for consultation on the book design, format, and publishing process.

Introduction

We live in a world where the pace of change and information sharing increases in order of magnitude everyday. The increase in cost of resources, population growth, prevalence of instantaneous global communication, onset of climate change and other factors are changing the nature of how people live their lives and what services and products are required to support civilization.

Due to the increase in pace and magnitude of change, organizations in every sector and industry are forced to change the way they operate, and the makeup of the services and products being offered. Organizations that change proactively, innovate first, and learn to ebb and flow with the waves of change will be the ones that survive and thrive.

Changes required to innovate may include: implementing a new strategic direction, merging with another organization, organizational restructuring, developing new services or products, reducing costs, increasing the efficiency of the supply chain, overall transformation to modernize the organization, and many others.

When planning for change, organizations often focus on the desired solution or change, while paying little regard to the fundamental assumptions driving the change, the organization's capability to change, and thoroughly preparing for the change in order to increase the likelihood of success.

Unchecked assumptions create blindspots and oversight that can result in failed change efforts. This paper provides guidance on how to thoughtfully develop and implement an organizational change strategy. See Table 1 for an overview of the sections of this paper.

Table 1. Overview of the Sections

Section	Description
Introduction	Overview and the need for planned change.
Section 1. Creating a Foundation for the Change Process	Guidance on how to check assumptions and best focus a change effort.
Section 2. Process for Leading Change	Threes stages for leading a change process.
Section 3. Critical Success Factors for Successful Change	Factors that increase the effectiveness of the change process and likelihood of successful change.
Section 4. Special Considerations for Leading Change Related to Sustainability	Points to consider when leading a change process that has a sustainability focus.
Conclusion	Change must be managed for it to succeed.
Appendix	Resources for leading change.

Section 1. Creating a Foundation for the Change Process

When organizations lack a well-planned change management process the chance of successful change is 35%, but doubles to 70% when a company engages in an effective change management process, according to a 2015 study by the Project Management Institute[1] and a 2010 study by McKinsey[2].

Organizational change management is the process of leading an organization or larger collection of people through a planned change process – providing a roadmap to plan, initiate and stabilize change. This process integrates organizational/corporate strategy, management processes, and collaboration between divisions within the organization.

One of the biggest flaws in change initiatives is making the wrong changes. Before a change process is embarked on, the fundamental assumptions that are the impetus of change must be examined and confirmed– including the challenge/problem, the overarching organizational/business strategy, stakeholder input and related areas. Establishing a stable foundation for change and anchoring the change process to it will increase the likelihood of achieving successful change and realizing the intended value (see Figure 1 on the following page).

---

[1]http://www.pmi.org/learning/pulse.aspx
[2]http://www.mckinsey.com/insights/organization/what_successful_transformations_share_mckinsey_global_survey_results

Figure 1. Foundation for the Change Process

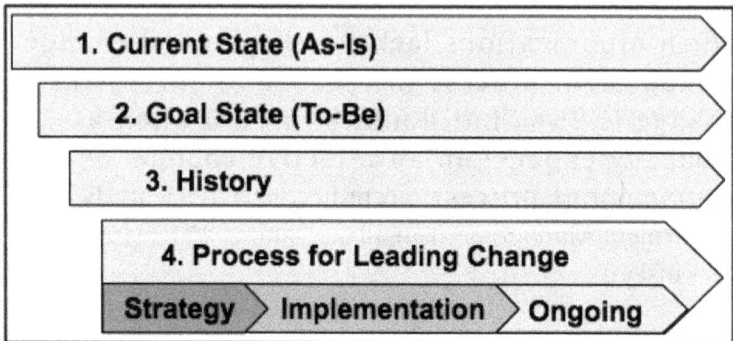

1. Current State (As-Is)

2. Goal State (To-Be)

3. History

4. Process for Leading Change

Strategy	Implementation	Ongoing

As preparation for planning change, the following four-step process is suggested to ground the change upon a stable foundation.

1.1 Current State (As-Is)

The current state of the organization must be assessed and understood. The areas to assess and level of detail will depend on the nature of the change project or initiative being considered. When preparing for a potential change the organization's current organizational/business process, communication process, training methods, and methods for sharing information must be understood— in order to integrate them into the change process later on.

In addition, before the direction for change can be determined or pursued, the underlying challenge that the change intends to address must be examined. Organizations often charge in the wrong direction, failing to examine the underlying assumptions of the challenge or problem they are trying to solve. Starting with the solution avoids examining core questions that underlie the way problems and solutions are approached, ignoring possibly false assumptions, and decreasing the likelihood that the new direction is the best course of action. This can lead to focusing on the wrong challenges and wrong solutions to the challenge. When organizations are faced with new challenges, such as, coping with climate change and sustainability, an examination of core questions is required in order to determine the right solutions.

To support the process of determining the root challenge or problem a specific working session(s) should be allocated to discussing the challenges among key stakeholders impacted by the challenge.

At the company Toyota when there is a problem they apply the "5 Why's". The "5 Why's" is a way of determining the root cause of a problem. For example, if the problem is a car defect, a team member asks, "*Well, why is there a defect?*". Then a team member replies to each answer with the question, "*Well, why is that?*". Then one continues to ask "why" to determine the root problem, peeling back deeper layers of the issue. These questions may lead the group to realize that they have not arrived at the root problem, nor the solution. This exercise often makes apparent any underlying assumptions. Examining the underlying assumptions and rationale for a given change can help reveal the questions and answers needed to arrive at the root problem and best solution.

1.2 Goal State (To-Be)

The goal state (to-be) must be supported by a business case showing that the cost and time required to achieve the change are justified. The business case provides detailed identification, quantification and timing of expected financial and other business benefits (justifications) derived from implementing the project.

> *"A critical factor for success is a robust business case that explains how to mitigate risks and quantify opportunities that could be achieved if the shared vision is realized."*
> *– Bob Willard*
>
> Bob Willard is a leading expert on the business value of corporate sustainability strategies. He served for 34 years at IBM focusing on business and leadership development. He emphasizes proactively avoiding risks and capturing opportunities associated with environmental issues.
>
> Internal and external data are used to craft a compelling justification for change. Market forces and relevant stakeholders that influence the organization's direction need to described. The case for change should be phrased in terms of risks, issues, and opportunities.
>
> The greatest bottom-line benefits of sustainability are increased employee productivity, increased operating efficiency, increased revenue/market share, and decreased insurance/borrowing costs.
>
> (Excerpt from Willard, B. (2009), *The Sustainability Champion's Guidebook: How to Transform Your Company*, New Society Publishers, Gabriola Island.)

In addition to the business case, it is important to create a road map for how the project will be implemented, how organizational change will be managed, and the critical steps needed to gain approval/support for the project. Senior leaders within the organization will be best informed on whether to approve the project or not, if the business case and road map are clear, a valid argument for the change is presented, and the path forward is described well.

1.3 History

The culture of an organization is the pattern of beliefs, values and learned ways of coping with experience that have developed during the course of an organization's history[3]. The history of the organization must be understood before embarking on a change process. Areas to review and understand include:

- Lessons learned from previous successful and unsuccessful change projects/initiatives
- Typical areas of resistance to change
- The core values of the organization
- Other projects, initiatives and changes that are occurring at the present time in the organization that may impact the success of a new change project being planned

The process for leading change is the core of organizational change management. The following section describes a three-phase process comprised of (1) strategy, (2) implementation and (3) ongoing.

---

[3] Brown, A. (1995), *Organisational Culture,* Pitman Publishing, London.

Section 2. Process for Leading Change

The purpose of Organizational Change Management is to guide organizations to accept and integrate changes that must be made to improve performance or meet desired organizational objectives. The process must address all human, cultural, policy, system, structure, and process related changes to the organization.

The organizational change process builds the:
- Successful implementation of an initiative, project or organization-wide change
- Awareness, understanding and commitment to reasons why the change(s) is needed
- Enhanced leadership capability to support the To-Be (goal) state
- Support required to continue the process of change, enabling it to integrate into daily operations
- Structured activities to identify and manage organizational impacts and risks
- Human capabilities to perform new roles and tasks
- Culture needed to accept and support the desired changes

Figure 2 on the following page illustrates a high-level process for leading change within an organization. There are three phases. Each phase builds on the previous phase. For smaller change efforts less activities are needed. As the scale of change increases more change activities are needed to lead the organization in the right direction. The Appendix has a Gantt chart with additional details.

Figure 2. Process for Leading Change

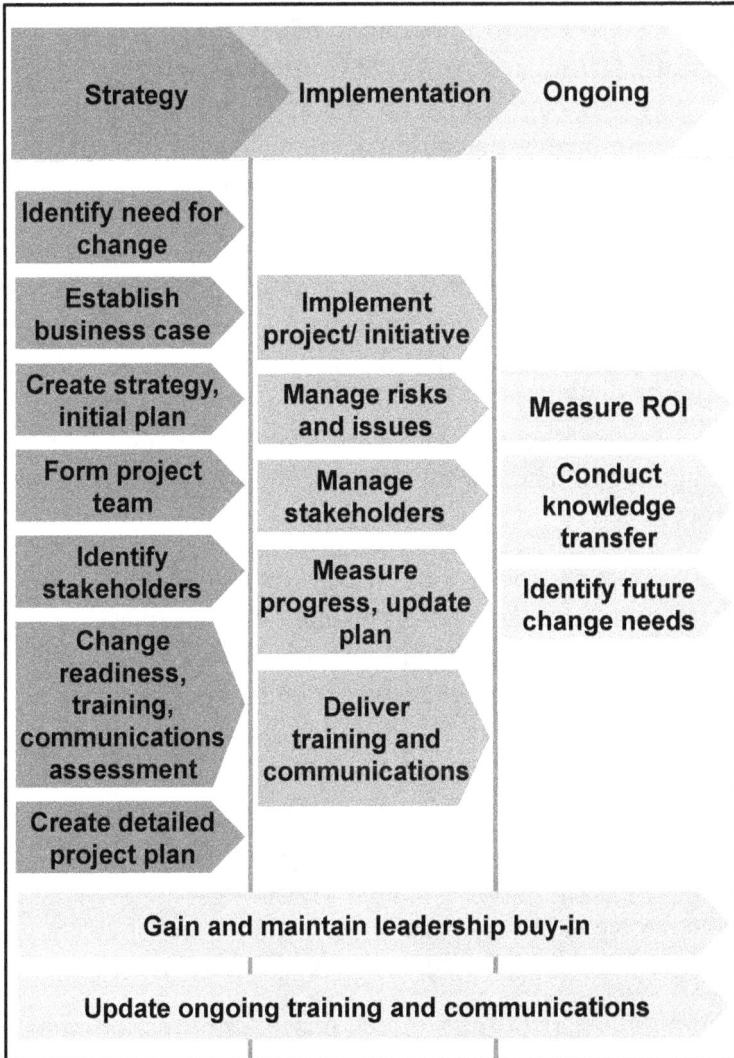

Strategy	Implementation	Ongoing
Identify need for change		
Establish business case	Implement project/ initiative	
Create strategy, initial plan	Manage risks and issues	Measure ROI
Form project team	Manage stakeholders	Conduct knowledge transfer
Identify stakeholders	Measure progress, update plan	Identify future change needs
Change readiness, training, communications assessment	Deliver training and communications	
Create detailed project plan		

Gain and maintain leadership buy-in

Update ongoing training and communications

2.1 Strategy

A strategy is a pattern of behavior over time that sets direction, focuses effort, defines the organization, and provides consistency[4]. In short, strategy provides a course of action. This phase includes preparing for the project/initiative, realizing the need for change, establishing the business case, and creating the strategy for change.

Having metrics in place to drive change in the right direction is a critical success factor. Throughout the change process it is important to verify that the intended results and benefits are being achieved. When there is a lack of progress and results, new or enhanced tactics must be applied to increase the effectiveness of the change process.

At the start of a project the first assessment is to determine the stakeholders impacted by the project including the level of impact to each stakeholder, how critical each stakeholder is to change success, and feedback on the success factors for the project. Other important assessments are change readiness (see Appendix for sample questions), communication needs, training needs, communication effectiveness, knowledge transfer needs, impacts to organizational/business processes, benefits realization, project progress, and related areas— each to be utilized on an as needed basis.

Planning is part of the strategy phase. Information and knowledge must be collected and analyzed about the scale of impacts to the organization in order to create a

---

[4] Mintzberg, H., Ahlstrand, B. and Lampel, J. (1998), *Strategy Safari: A Guided Tour Through the Wilds of Strategic Management,* Free Press, New York.

detailed plan. Planning involves determining what activities need to occur, when they need to occur, who is responsible, and what the cost will be for each area of work. Milestones serve as completion points for major pieces of work or the mark of phase completion. Plans need to be updated and reported on a regular basis. It is common to report weekly progress and update the project plan as needed. In addition to tracking progress, risks and issues must be tracked, reported and mitigated throughout the project.

2.2 Implementation

Implementation is the phase when the work described in the strategy and plan are carried out. During this phase the solution, communications, training and related activities are delivered. The project plan should be tracked and updated on a weekly, or on an as needed basis. Risks and issues must be tracked and mitigated throughout implementation in a formal manner. The effectiveness of the plan and the activities being implemented must be measured. Based on what is working well and areas that need to be improved, the project/initiative change plan should be updated. Regularly adjusting the approach to organizational change management based on feedback increases the likelihood of successful change and realizing the intended benefits.

In addition to the core activities related to carrying out the solution, stakeholder expectations and organizational culture must be fostered. Expectation setting is often carried out by a variety of communication mechanisms and trainings— in-person meetings, electronic communications (email, social media, webpage, video), road shows, events, newsletters, conference calls and related mechanisms.

2.3 Ongoing

At the end of the implementation phase and the start of the ongoing phase all documentation is archived for future reference, knowledge is transferred from the project implementers to the operating employees (as needed), and the realization of benefits are measured (aka ROI). In some cases it can take months to years to determine if the return on investment (ROI) was fully realized or not. For example, if the goal of a project were to increase the energy efficiency of a manufacturing plant by 5% per year, it would take 1 year to verify the benefits are being realized. It is important when measuring the benefits realized to account for both tangible benefits (usually money saved or earned) and intangible benefits, such as, new knowledge, innovation, increased performance, enhanced reputation, and related areas.

At the completion of the project lessons learned from the project/initiative implementation should be documented for ongoing adoption of the change and to support knowledge sharing for future projects. An activity that can be performed in parallel is identifying future organizational change needs.

Continuing support is often needed for projects or initiatives (aka ongoing support, hence the name of the phase). This may be in the form of continuing to deliver communications and training related to the new project. Before the completion of the project the changes and resulting new responsibilities must be integrated into standard organizational processes (or a plan to do so must be developed and implemented).

Section 3: Critical Success Factors for Successful Change

The field of organizational change management (based on organizational science) provides many case studies, principles, critical success factors (CSFs) and lessons learned that inform how to carry out organizational change. It is both an art and science. There are best practices to follow, although it takes experience to learn how to implement them. For that reason it is optimal to lead change using a team of leaders that can support one another, and leverage each others' experience and capabilities.

This section describes CSFs and levers for implementing change within organizations. These suggestions are based on the author's experience from leading several large-scale change projects and initiatives, and from having completed a doctoral dissertation examining the role or organizational change in sustainability[5]— see Appendix for bio.

3.1 Why Some Organizations Succeed at Changing While Others Do Not

When organizations fail at implementing a new project or initiative it is usually due to a poorly managed change process, lack of adequate funding, or lack of leadership support. Nearly two decades ago in Kotter's landmark article[6], *"Leading Change: Why Transformation Efforts*

---

[5] Holliday, S. (2010), "A Case Study of How DuPont Reduced Its Envir. Footprint: The Role of Org. Change in Sustainability", Washington, D.C., George Washington University, p. 193.

[6] Kotter, J. (1995), "Leading Change: Why Transformation Efforts Fail", *Harvard Business Review*, Vol. 73 No. 2, pp. 59-67.

Fail", he described eight reasons why change efforts fail (see Figure 3). His insights are still true today.

In order to avoid these pitfalls it is important to adhere to a well thought out organizational change process. Skipping steps or phases of the change process often leads to increased costs or change failure. A typical step that is not given enough importance is engaging all the critical stakeholders early on. Starting a conversation with critical stakeholders provides insight into how to design and lead the change process.

The art and science of organizational change management provides many tactics to avoid the pitfalls described in Figure 3. The next section describes eleven CSFs for achieving organizational change. Throughout the change process these CSFs must be applied during the change process in order to direct change in the right ways and gain adoption of the change.

Figure 3. Why Transformation Efforts Fail

1. Not establishing a great enough sense of urgency
2. Not creating a powerful enough guiding coalition
3. Lacking a vision
4. Undercommunicating the vision by a factor of ten
5. Not removing obstacles to the new vision
6. Not systematically planning for and creating short-term wins
7. Declaring victory too soon
8. Not anchoring changes in the organization's culture

"The single biggest error people make when trying to change is lacking a sense of urgency."
— John Kotter

John Kotter is regarded by many as the authority on leadership and change. He has authored eighteen books to date— twelve of them bestsellers. Over the past thirty years, his articles in The Harvard Business Review (HBR) have sold more reprints than any of the hundreds of distinguished authors who have written for that publication during that time period.

Organizations often become complacent resting on their laurels due to a satisfaction with past successes. In order for organizations to initiate and succeed at change, a high sense of urgency and a low sense of complacency are both needed.

In order for this to occur, either an external force (e.g., competition, economic downturn, regulatory change) or internal force (e.g., making the case for change) must foster a sense of urgency to trigger action. Applying internal force to foster urgency is based on makings risks and opportunities clear, realizing the desire to win now, and creating a focus on the need to change.

(Excerpt from Kotter, J. (2008), *A Sense of Urgency*, Harvard University Press, Boston.)

3.2 Eleven CSFs for Organizational Change

Based on knowledge gained while serving as a Senior Organizational Change Management and Strategy consultant at IBM Global Business Services and doctoral research on organizational change, there are eleven CSFs (Critical Success Factors) for implementing organizational change. Determining which areas/levers to apply depends on the nature of the change, the organizational culture, and the complexity of the change. Intentionally incorporating the CSFs into the change management plan makes the change more impactful and likely to succeed (see Table 2).

Table 2. CSFs for Organizational Change

Area	Description
Gaining Leadership Buy-In	The most important critical success factor
Establishing Change Champion	Leadership for the initiative/project
Establishing Change Network	Hub of two-way communications (send/gather information)
Engaging Stakeholders	Identify, engage and manage stakeholders
Making case for Benefit vs. Cost	Must be a business case (ROI)
Part of Larger Initiative	For a change to be permanent it must be part of a larger program or aligned to the strategic goals of the organization

Area	Description
Apply Two-Way Communications	Throughout the organization and externally for reinforcement
Organizational Change Assessment(s)	Of current behavior and attitudes, areas of improvement, training needs, progress of initiative, results
Training	Formal, structured training and informal by example
Rewards/ Incentives	Monetary, recognition, part of annual performance appraisal
External Support	Use external training and consulting to kick-start and guide

3.3 The Prerequisite to Change is Effective Leadership and Management

Organizations depend on *systems* (mechanisms for information exchange between people and organizational units), *structures* (reporting relationships between people and organizational units) and *processes* (interactions between people and groups) in order to function[7]. For an organization to be effective and successful it must have mechanisms to enable management and leadership. A perquisite for organizations to be effective at managing change is having an effective organization in the first place.

---

[7] The concept of systems, structures and processes is based on advice from and several documents created by Charles Krone while he served as an advisor to DuPont.

"Senior executive support is not always possible. Sometimes the best we can achieve is non-objection." - Chad O. Holliday, Jr.

Chad Holliday is the Founder and Managing Partner of EMWS. He is the former Chairman of the Board and Chief Executive Officer of DuPont, 1998-2008. He is currently on the boards of C2HMHill, Royal Dutch Shell, Deere & Co., Bank of America, and Global Federation of Competitiveness Councils. He is Chair of the Executive Committee for United Nations Sustainable Energy for All.

It is ideal to have senior management buy-in for an organizational change initiative or project. In some cases official support or endorsement is not possible. In those cases non-objection to the change is all that can be achieved.

The role of middle level management is to direct the day-to-day operations of an organization. Middle level management often best understands how the organizational can be more effective, and must implement those changes in order to maintain the organization. When non-objection is the only approval for the change, buy-in for the change does not occur until the results are proven.

(Based on personal conversation on September 12, 2013.)

One myth in leadership is that a singular heroic leader is needed within an organization for its change process to succeed[8]. There are two problems with depending on a heroic leader. First, if the change fails, the organization may place the majority of the blame on the single leader and assume that if a new heroic leader is appointed, change will then be successful. Second, and on a related note, it is false to think that one person ever leads change. Successful adoption of change is the responsibility of the entire organization and is often led by a cross-functional team that has tie-ins to various key departments within the organization.

Although it is true the buy-in and support of top leadership is needed, leadership is a phenomenon that occurs throughout the levels and divisions of an organization. Leaders hold the vision for an organization and sustain the organization. Leaders drive the organization to achieve its goals. In many leading organizations leaders strive to maintain a creative tension where there is synchronicity between pressure, innovation and success.

When it comes to enabling successful change, leadership and management can often oppose one another. Leadership may push for change, while management tries to maintain control of the status quo. Leadership and management must work together to drive the desired change. Table 3 on the follow page describes a few typical areas of responsibility for management and leadership in order to show the contrast. Management processes are controlling mechanisms that are put in place to create

---

[8] Senge et. al. (1999), *The Dance of Change: The Challenge of Sustaining Momentum in Learning Organizations,* Doubleday, New York.

Table 3. Management Versus Leadership Mechanisms

Management	Leadership
• Human Resource Management • Organizational/ Business Strategy Development and Goal Setting • Financial Management • Customer Service Management • Operations Management	• Strategy and Goal Setting • Cultivating Values and Culture • Service and Product Innovation • Mitigating Risks and Ceasing Opportunities • Engaging Diverse Stakeholders

the desired functions within the organization. Leadership processes are put in place to provide direction and inspiration. Suddenly when a new project, initiative or strategic direction is put in place there is a strong leadership focus on achieving the desired outcome. A conflict is created when the management mechanisms go unchanged. Leadership seeks to inspire change, while management tries to reinforce desired outcomes and behaviors of the past.

3.4 Suggestions for Building a Change Leadership Team

For larger change initiatives, such as ones that impact the majority of the organization, it is important to have a dedicated team to lead the change project/initiative. Responsibilities of the change management team include delivering all of the activities described in the change strategy and plan. The team should be comprised of

"Mechanisms designed to increase motivation can dampen it." – *Daniel Pink*

Daniel H. Pink is the author of five provocative bestselling books about the changing world of work. He bases his recommendations on 50 years of behavioral science to overturn the conventional wisdom about human motivation and offer a more effective path to high performance.

Greater monetary rewards do incent people to perform better on routine tasks. Although, when it comes to cognitive tasks simply giving people greater monetary rewards decreases performance. In order to increase performance on cognitive tasks three elements are needed:

(1) *Autonomy–* the desire to direct our own lives

(2) *Mastery–* the urge to make progress and get better at something that matters

(3) *Purpose–* the yearning to do what we do in the service of something larger than ourselves

(Excerpt from Pink, D. (2011), *Drive: The Surprising Truth About What Motivates Us,* Riverhead Books, New York.)

people that a have formal connection (per the organizational chart or structure) to various parts of the organization. For example, a 2012 study by the National Association of Environmental Managers found that the majority of teams that lead sustainability strategy, planning, measurement and reporting are cross-functional. Within the cross-functional teams departments represented often include: corporate communications, operations, legal, sales, marketing; and Environment, Health and Safety (EHS).[9] Having a cross-functional team allows the change project/initiative to have a deep reach within the organization, best understand stakeholder concerns, and understand cultural issues that may affect change success.

3.5 Avoid Crashing a Project/ Initiative

The Gartner Hype Cycle[10] provides a depiction of how excitement can be created about an idea, then steeply decline or crash. The Hype Cycle was designed to represent the maturity, adoption and social application of specific technologies. Figure 4 on the following page applies the Hype Cycle to change adoption. At any point along the Hype Cycle an idea, service or product can fail. Often there are overinflated expectations about a new project/initiative (point B). Overtime a project will fail if results are not delivered or if support is lost due to lack of realistic expectation setting (point C). If the benefits of a project are realized (point D), there is an increase in the adoption of change (point E).

---

[9] NAEM (2012), *"EHS & Sustainability Staffing and Structure Benchmark Report"*, Washington, D.C., National Association of Environmental Managers.

[10] http://en.wikipedia.org/wiki/File:Gartner_Hype_Cycle.svg

Figure 4. Gartner Hype Cycle Applied to Poor Change Adoption

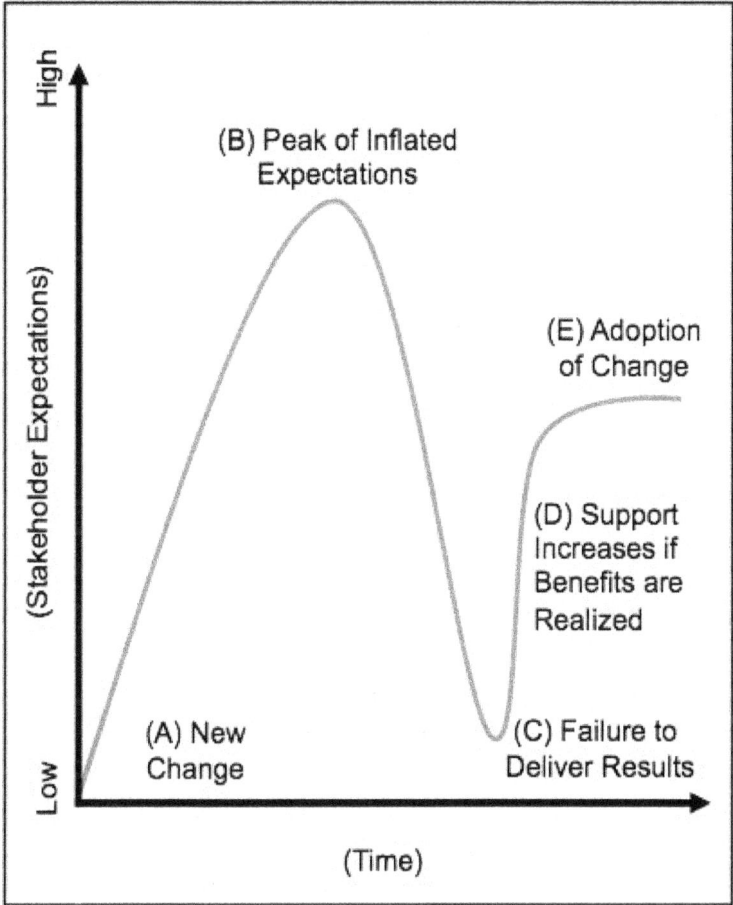

Figure 4. Gartner Hype Cycle Applied to Poor Change Adoption

3.6 Increasing Acceptance through Change Management

When effective organizational change management is applied to projects the likelihood of success and adoption of the change is increased. Figure 5 illustrates how the level of stakeholder buy-in and overall change success increases or decreases overtime, depending on whether or not change management is utilized effectively. Problems often arise when the complexity of the change becomes apparent leading to decreased acceptance of the change(s), disappointment, and possibly despair over the money and time lost over the failing project. When effective organizational change management is applied expectations are kept in check and the project/initiative is kept on track, leading to the highest likelihood of change success.

When an organization undergoes a specific change communications and training are typically used to direct change in the right way. It is a mistake to simply rely on training and communications (surface engagement) and expect people to change. Deep engagement is needed in order to change the way the organization operates and behaves. Organizational change management/ leadership focuses on engaging deep aspects of the organization including the subtleties within culture, systems, structures and processes.

Figure 5. Change Curve: With vs. Without Organizational Change Management[11]

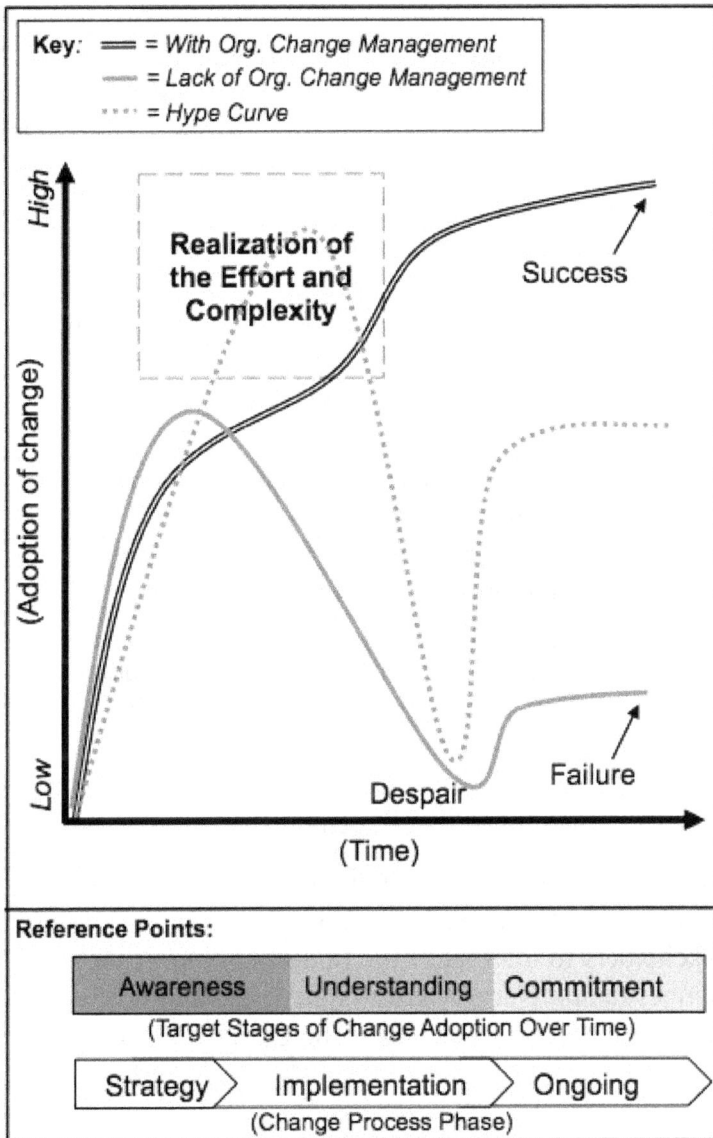

Key: ▬▬ = With Org. Change Management
      ▬▬ = Lack of Org. Change Management
      ····· = Hype Curve

High (Adoption of change) Low

Realization of the Effort and Complexity

Success

Despair   Failure

(Time)

Reference Points:

Awareness	Understanding	Commitment

(Target Stages of Change Adoption Over Time)

Strategy	Implementation	Ongoing

(Change Process Phase)

---

[11] Based on collective work of Darryl Conner, e.g., Conner, D. (2006), *Managing At the Speed of Change: How Resilient Managers Succeed and Prosper Where Others Fail,* Random House, New York.

3.7 Stages of Change Adoption

During the course of a project or initiative the objectives of the organizational change management process are to deliver the intended benefits of the project/ initiative, maximize acceptance of the change by stakeholders, and embed the changes within the culture, systems, structures and processes of the organization. Organizational change management drives the level of stakeholder adoption of the change during the change process. Figure 6 on the following page depicts three stages of change adoption. These three stages are the core of how human behavior related to a change should be directed in order to gain adoption of a given organizational change.

Awareness- The first stage of change adoption is awareness. The objective of this stage is for stakeholders to know what the change is, why it is needed and the main areas of the organization that will change.

Understanding- The second stage of change adoption is understanding. The objective of this stage is for stakeholders to realize the direct impacts to their department and job, and what their role is in supporting the successful adoption of the change(s).

Commitment- The third stage of change adoption is commitment. The objective of this stage is for stakeholders to internalize the understanding of the changes taking place, realize the benefits, and want to be part of creating and stabilizing the change.

Figure 6. Stages of Change Adoption[12]

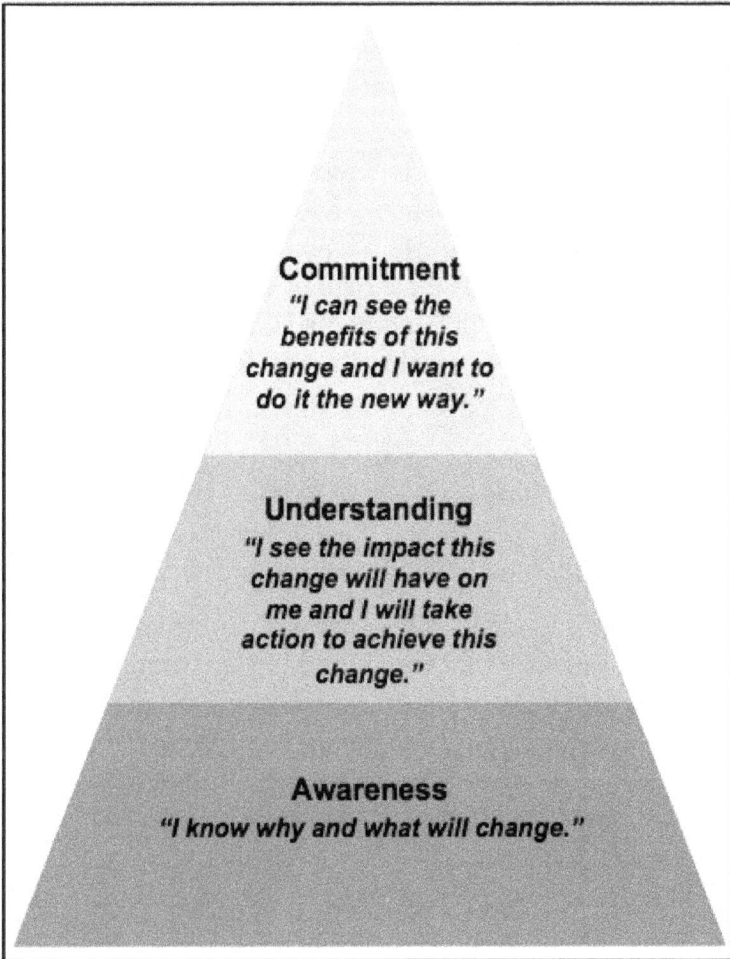

Commitment
"I can see the benefits of this change and I want to do it the new way."

Understanding
"I see the impact this change will have on me and I will take action to achieve this change."

Awareness
"I know why and what will change."

---

[12] Based on personal experience and collective work of Darryl Conner.

"In order to co-create dynamic change within an organization, it must be ignited by a shift in the way individuals think, feel, and behave. The first step toward this shift is practicing awareness."

– Clyde Croswell

Clyde Croswell is a writer, consultant and professor of organizational science, leadership and qualitative research. He served for 29 years in the Marines, retiring as a Lieutenant Colonel. One of his roles was conducting and administering Marine Corps bands. He uses his abilities and experience to cultivate awareness in others.

Awareness is noticing patterns of thought, behavior, action, and relationships. An increase in one's ability to be aware does not occur on its own. It must be learned through practice.

In order to engage people in an organization to better understand, commit to and support a given change, the change must be related to the actions, behaviors, thoughts and emotions of those affected. This is achieved through authentic two-way communication where the positive and negative perceptions of the change are allowed to surface. Those affected by the change must be involved in assessing the affect of change in order to gain their active participation in enacting change over time as change supporters and leaders.

(Based on Croswell, C. V. and Holliday, S. B. (2004), "The New Science of Awareness: Triggering the Emergence of Consciousness in Living Systems", *The International Journal of Knowledge, Culture and Change Management*, Vol. 4 No. 1, pp. 1619-1626.)

Section 4: Special Considerations for Leading Change Related to Sustainability

In an organizational context, sustainability can be defined as a strategy, and set of values and practices for innovating the way organizations use energy and resources, manage impacts to communities and society, and manage their environmental footprint.

The factors to consider for effective organizational change for sustainability are fundamentally the same as effective organizational change for any other purpose. These common factors include: leadership buy-in, strategic organizational alignment, two-way communications, stakeholder engagement, organizational restructuring, training, incentives, organizational change facilitation, and developing an organizational change network. What should be highlighted about organizational change for sustainability is the great difficulty of the challenges being faced by all organizations and societies: population increase, global warming, depletion of fossil fuels, rising energy costs, rapid growth of developing countries, and economic fragility. Another difficulty of organizational change toward sustainability is that for some organizations, the gap between the current state (As-Is) and the desired state (To-Be) of a sustainable organization may be huge. The costs for this change to be undertaken must be absorbed incrementally or else the expense may be too great for the organization to continue operating.

It is also important to consider the costs of inaction. For many changes the expense of change increases manifold as it is delayed. For example, in terms of investing in energy efficiency, the International Energy Agency estimates that every dollar invested in energy today saves four dollars by the year 2030. A way to strengthen the business case for change is to project the ROI over a ten-year or longer time span.

4.1 External Forces Driving Organizational Change

The following are three external forces or trends that are driving change within organizations. There are a multitude of other forces impacting organizations varying by sector and industry. This section serves as a snapshot to set the context for considering the role of organizational change as it relates to sustainability.

1. **Finite resources being depleted.** Various finite resources are constantly being consumed or utilized, resulting in their decrease, e.g., fossil fuels, metals, food, and potable water. Technology may help us discover more quantities of resources. Although it is critical to develop renewable sources of energy and materials that make use of resources we use every day to operate organizations and carryon life.

   Population increase causes resources to be depleted further, increasing the price of resources, resulting in greater inequality, disruption of supply chains, and an extreme lack of resources for basic human needs in the least developed areas of the world. As countries increase in wealth the tendency is for the population to consume more food and consumer goods, exacerbating depletion of resources.

2. **Instantaneous Global Connectivity-** Big data is available for most aspects of life. In the span of two days humanity now produces more data than it had from the dawn of civilization to the year 2003[13]. Within the next four years the amount of data will double (by 2017). Understanding how to use this data to drive business and organizational success and be good stewards of society will be an ongoing learning experience for individuals and organizations. Due to this global instantaneous connectivity the lines between local, domestic and multinational business are blurred, forcing all organizations to continuously evolve and reinvent themselves.

3. **Climate Change.** Due to increasing levels of carbon, the earth's climate is being altered. Civilization continues to operate at unsustainable levels where too much Carbon is emitted into the atmosphere. The primary impacts are overall temperature increase of the oceans and the atmosphere, increasing acidity of oceans from higher concentrations of dissolved $CO2$ disrupting ecosystems, increased frequency and intensity of storms, rising sea levels from melting of arctic ice, drought in some areas, flooding in other areas, extreme weather events, disruption of natural cycles for plant growth, extinction of vulnerable animal and plant species. The secondary impacts create the risks and opportunities to organizations and civilization that vary greatly by sector, industry and geographic location.

---

[13] Smolna, R. and Erwitt, J. (2012), *The Human Face of Big Data,* Against All Odds Productions, New York.

4.2 Operational Sustainability Framework

Within organizations, sustainability is often considered in terms of the triple-bottom-line (TBL) of social, environmental, and economic values; akin to environment and social corporate governance (ESG)[14]. Organizations often muddle these areas and are unable to align these values to systems, structures, and processes due to the difficulty of defining strategy, setting goals, and measuring performance. The most effective way to consider sustainability is to apply an operational framework of sustainability to organizations' operations, and services and products (see Figure 7 on the following page).

Organizational change toward sustainability often involves new and confusing challenges to organizations. In order to successfully transform an organization to be more sustainable, organizational change management is required. Because of the need to include environmental footprint reduction as part of organizational strategy, a greater understanding of organizational change as it relates to environmental footprint reduction is needed to help leaders and managers develop, implement, and following through with organizational transformation strategies.

---

[14] Savitz, A. (2013), *Talent, Transformation, and the Triple Bottom Line: How Companies Can Leverage Human Resources to Achieve Sustainable Growth*, Jossey-Bass, San Francisco.

Figure 7. Operational Sustainability Framework

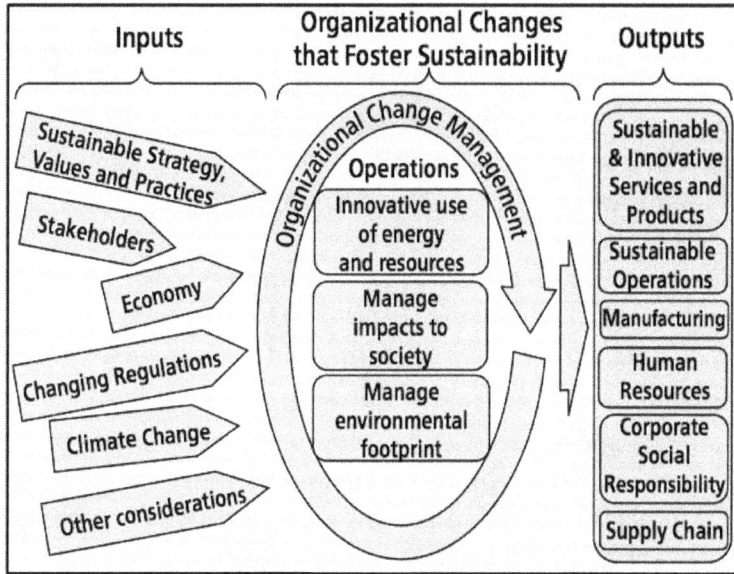

Figure 7. Operational Sustainability Framework

Inputs
- Sustainable Strategy, Values and Practices
- Stakeholders
- Economy
- Changing Regulations
- Climate Change
- Other considerations

Organizational Changes that Foster Sustainability

Organizational Change Management
- Operations
- Innovative use of energy and resources
- Manage impacts to society
- Manage environmental footprint

Outputs
- Sustainable & Innovative Services and Products
- Sustainable Operations
- Manufacturing
- Human Resources
- Corporate Social Responsibility
- Supply Chain

4.3 Four Recommendation for Applying Organizational Change to Sustainability

Based on Holliday's (2010) doctoral dissertation research[15] of the actions, decisions, interactions, and operations undertaken by DuPont from 1989 to 2008 that enabled it to transform into a sustainable organization the following section describes four recommendations for applying organizational change management to sustainability.

As background, DuPont was described in 1989 – by both Greenpeace and the U.S. Environmental Protection Agency – as one of the worst polluters in the United States.

---

[15] Published as a doctoral dissertation in 2010 and as a book in 2011. Holliday, S. (2011). *A Case Study of How DuPont Reduced Its Environment Footprint: The Role of Organizational Change in Sustainability.* LAP Lambert Academic Publishing: Saarbrücken.

DuPont reacted to that burning platform and embarked on a path toward sustainability. Each year since then DuPont has strived to raise its bar and proactively change. Since 1990, DuPont shifted its product line from being 100 percent chemically-based, to 70 percent chemically-based and 30 percent bio-based materials; and reduced it greenhouse gas emissions (GHGs) 72 percent, mainly through waste reduction and water/energy efficiency.

Recommendation 1: Organizational Sustainability Should Include Operations, Products and Services, and Social Responsibility

Because of the long time frame required for developing products and services, organizational/business strategy for sustainability must be considered proactively[16]. Aspects of that proactive planning process include determining the customers' future needs for sustainable products and services. Those needs should direct research and development, sales and marketing, and the timing for making these new products available. The company providing products and services may have to employ organizational change in order to align its operations and products and services to meet the customers' future needs.

Organizational/business strategy is nonlinear in nature and has to be linked to organizational change. The fundamental way in which an organization affects individuals and other organizations is through its products and services. As a result, for an organization to be sustainable, its products and services must be sustainable.

---

[16] Mintzberg, H. and Waters, J. A. (1983), "The mind of the strategist", in Srivastva, S. (Ed.) *The executive mind*, Jossey-Bass, San Francisco, pp. 58-83.

"It appears to be an environmental footprint story, but the real transformation going on in DuPont has to do with the societal value of the products and services." – Paul Tebo

From 1993 to 2004, Paul Tebo served as the V.P. of Environmental, Health and Safety at DuPont. He was a sustainability officer at DuPont before the term was coined. During an interview in 2009, Paul mentioned that one of the main contributions DuPont makes to society is providing services and products that support people to live healthier, be more productive and contribute to the sustainable of our planet.

One of the ways DuPont provides more value to its customers without increasing its environmental footprint is through services. DuPont has the largest safety consulting business in the world, where it trains companies how to assess and implement best practices for safety. This notion of training as a service has been extended to other areas, e.g., building energy efficiency and materials efficiency.

(Excerpt from Holliday, S. (2010), "A Case Study of How DuPont Reduced Its Environment Footprint: The Role of Organizational Change in Sustainability", *Human Resource Development*, Washington, D.C., The George Washington University p. 193.)

From the time an organization has the initial creative idea for a new product or service to the time the product or service is actually developed and made market ready may be several years (as with the case of DuPont). With the current (as of 2013) shifts occurring in environmental legislation (including carbon constraints) and rise in the cost of both energy and natural resources, in the coming years there will be an increasingly stronger business case for sustainable products and services. This indicates that when formulating an organizational/business strategy for the coming year, research and development and related planning must be more innovative and sustainable than the current customer or market needs. When organizational change is in alignment with the strategy, considerations for helping organizational leaders and other employees to cope with change must be proactive. Then, as product and service development and delivery are realigned to meet future needs, the people within the organization must also be aligned to that future orientation— including organizational structure, job roles, training, communications, knowledge sharing, strategy, and related areas.

Recommendation 2: Resistance to Organizational Change for Sustainability Presents Challenges and Opportunities

Resistance to organizational change can be defined as a negative emotional, cognitive, and intentional response to a change initiative[17]. Most employees' initial reaction to an organizational change initiative has some degree of

---

[17] Piderit, S. K. (2000), "Rethinking Resistance and Recognizing Ambivalence: A Multidimensional View of Attitudes Toward an Organizational Change", *Academy of Management Review*, Vol. 25 No. 4, pp. 783-794.

ambivalence, where there is a mixture of positive and negative reactions along in the areas of behavior, emotion, cognition, and intention. Allowing the causes behind the ambivalence to be examined and learned from can foster more successful change initiatives by generating new knowledge and new possibilities for understanding and action. Resistance to change that goes unaddressed can cause an organizational change initiative to be delayed, cost more, or fail.

Understanding and overcoming organizational resistance is required for organizational change to be effective in the long term regardless of whether an organization has a burning platform or not. When members of an organization are concerned about a new initiative, it is an opportunity to start a conversation. Through communication, information about the change effort can be exchanged and shared (e.g., in person, telephone call, workshop, newsletter, email, social media, webcast, or other forms). Two-way communications (e.g., a townhall style meeting) or assessments (e.g., interviews, focus groups, and surveys) facilitate learning about issues causing the resistance to change. Gathering and analyzing data about the issues causing resistance to organizational change may provide guidance for more effective ways to govern the initiative and generate new knowledge, new possibilities, and better outcomes[18].

---

[18] Pardo del Val, M. and Fuentes, C. (2003), "Resistance to change: A literature review and empirical study", *Management Decision,* Vol. 41 No. 2, pp. 148-155.

Recommendation 3: The Role of Senior Management—Including CEOs, Vice Presidents, and Other Executives—Is to Influence Organizational Change Toward Sustainability

Leadership support is one of the most widely recognized critical success factors in any organizational change effort[19]. One of the first steps for initiating organizational change for sustainability is to establish a network of sustainability change agents throughout the organization. First CEO support should be gained, then organizational unit support, by establishing a strategic change board or committee and working groups within each of the units (see Figure 8 on the following page).

At DuPont, the initial steps toward organizational sustainability were initiated by the then CEO, Ed Woolard, in 1989. Subsequently, CEO Chad Holliday made sustainability an intrinsic dimension of DuPont's mission, vision, and goals. Other key change champions included Bill Reilly (DuPont Board Member and former EPA Administrator), Paul Tebo (DuPont VP of Safety, Health, and Environment), Linda Fisher (DuPont VP of Safety, Health, and Environment and Chief Sustainability Officer), Dawn Rittenhouse (DuPont Director of Sustainability), and many others. At every level of the organization and in every unit, there must be accountability for integrating sustainability into the organization, including a board or committee for sustainability at the senior-most level of the organization and working groups within each unit.

---

[19] Kotter, J. P. (1996), *Leading Change,* Harvard Business School Press, Boston.

Figure 8. Recommended Organizational Change Network Levels

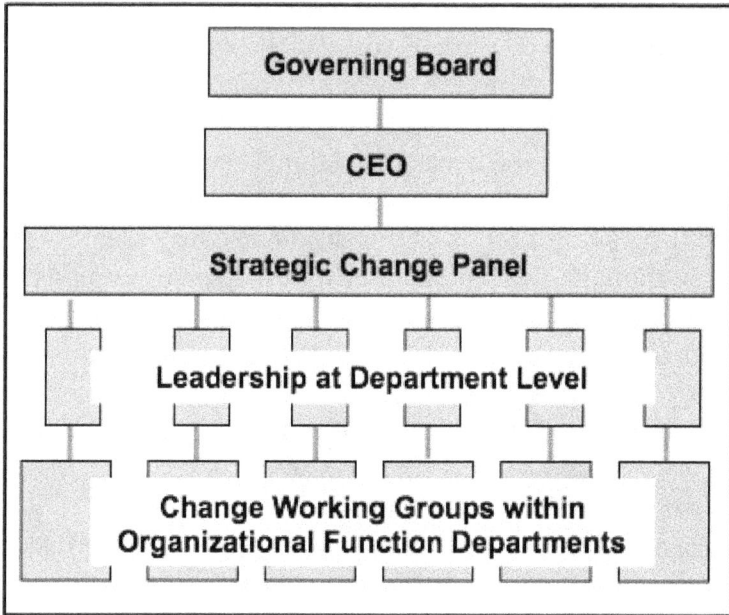

Recommendation 4: Stakeholders Must Be Involved in Organizational Change and Sustainability, and Their Current and Future Needs Must Be Understood

The most widely used definition of a stakeholder is "any individual or organization that affects or is affected by an organization"[20]. This definition can be extended to include all living things—a stakeholder is "any naturally occurring entity which affects or is affected by organizational performance"[21].

---

[20] Quote from p. 46 in Freeman, E. (1984), *Strategic Management: A Stakeholder Approach,* Pitman Publishing, Boston.

[21] Quote from p. 92 in Starik, M. (1994), "Essay by Mark Starik: The

The customer is the most important stakeholder of for-profit organizations. The customers' current and future needs in terms of sustainability are what drive the organization to develop its sustainability strategy and business model. Through constant, vigilant, direct, two-way communication with customers, feedback can be shared allowing the needs of customers in terms of services and products to be best understood. Developing products and services that are sustainable may require more thought and time than unsustainable products. As a result, to develop products and services that meet the future needs of customers, an organization must actively seek to understand what the customers' changing needs are now and will likely be in the future.

In the case of DuPont, sometimes customers were unaware that more sustainable products were needed. In those cases, DuPont often had to educate and convince customers that the new products and services would help their organization. In this sense, sales and marketing and research and development for sustainable products and services requires two-way communication—with the goals of organizational alignment and knowledge sharing between organizational levels and operating functions.

Toronto Conference: Reflections on Stakeholder Theory", *Business & Society,* Vol. 33 No. 1, pp. 89-95.

"Tipping points are created by influencers, and not simply an indiscriminate number of people gaining interest. Once a trend or behavior crosses a threshold it spreads like wildfire."

– Malcolm Gladwell

Malcolm Gladwell is a writer for *The New Yorker* and authored 4 best selling books, drawing from the fields of sociology, psychology, and social psychology. His work uncovers truths hidden in strange data. He says, *"There is more going on beneath the surface than we think, and more going on in little, finite moments of time than we would guess."*

A tipping is a moment of critical mass that, once it occurs, leads inevitably to a transformation. Gladwell found there elements in creating a tipping point:

(1) *The Law of the Few-* a small set of people are responsible for creating tipping points that have an ability to influence others (connectors, mavens and sales people).

(2) *The Stickiness Factor-* the content of a message must be impactful & memorable.

(3) *The Power of Context-* The external environment and culture of the social group(s) greatly effects behavior.

(Excerpt from Gladwell , M. (2000), *The Tipping Point: How Little Things Can Make a Big Difference* Little Brown, New York, and http://www.ted.com/speakers/malcolm _gladwell.html)

4.4 Organizational Change Management Applications for Sustainability

Organizational change toward sustainability can be such a challenge for most organizations that continuous realignment of the organizational change process and organizational/ business strategy may be required for successful change.

Several conditions should be met before an organization embarks on a sustainability project, initiative, program, or organization-wide transformation. The business case should be determined, leadership buy-in should be gained, a change network should be formed, communications should be developed, and impacts to the organization should be determined, among other factors.
Organizational change management champions, agents, or facilitators can support the change process. Table 4 on the following page describes some ways in which organizational change management can be specifically applied to sustainability.

Table 4. Organizational Change Management Applications for Sustainability

Management	Operations	Services and Products
• Working with organizational leaders to determine impacts, strategy, goals, metrics, reporting, and changes needed • Actionable road map for sustainability • Successful project delivery • Training for leaders and employees for sustainability and carbon-constraint thinking	• Behavioral change for energy, water, and other resource efficiency • Developing incentives and awards to foster sustainability thinking • Organizational transformation strategy • Return on investment planning and reporting	• Customer engagement strategy to determine service and product needs for sustainability • Cross-organizational department and cross-functional teaming and integration for innovation • Industry assessment to determine sustainability performance compared to competitors • Capability assessment for the current and future organization

Conclusion

In organizations and society, people often do not change until they are forced to, due to external circumstances. This is referred to as a "burning platform"— a situation where people are forced to act due to the alternative of not acting being worse[22]. In organizational change management literature, a similar phenomenon is a "disorienting dilemma"— an external or internal event that calls into question the deepest assumptions about the self and others[23].

The distinction between the two concepts is important to understand in order to best direct successful proactive change. Organizations often operate in a comfort zone and avoid innovating or increasing performance levels proactively. When a burning platform seems to be lacking people are reluctant to change. By creating a compelling story describing the need to change a disorienting dilemma can be presented, calling into question the status quo, describing the need to improve the organization in a particular dimension. When an entire organization is able to understand why there is a need to change, it is easier to contribute to and follow a plan for how to change.

A highly successful change agent who was able to change the control of a country through peaceful means was Mahatma Gandhi. In the early 20th century Gandhi once said, *"A technical society has two choices. First it can wait until catastrophic failures expose systematic deficiencies, distortion and deceptions... Secondly, a culture can*

---

[22] http://goo.gl/UQ1Zlb

[23] Mezirow, J. (1991), *Transformative Dimensions of Adult Learning*, Jossey-Bass, San Francisco.

provide social checks and balances to correct for systematic distortion prior to catastrophic failures. "[24] In other words every organization is forced to cope with change. We can cope with change reactively or proactively.

When change is enacted proactively using a planned process there is greater power to direct the change in the right direction with intended benefits. By effectively applying organizational change management the likelihood of achieving successful change increases from 35% to 70%.

---

[24] Khoshoo, T. N. (1995), *Mahatma Gandhi: An Apostle of Applied Human Ecology,* Tata Energy Research Institute, New Delhi.

Appendix

Sample Questions for Assessing the Foundation for the Change Process

- *Mission:* Is your mission clear, measurable and manageable?

- *Stakeholders:* Are you engaging diverse stakeholders in a quality way that brings new knowledge and capabilities into your organization?

- *Core Questions:* Are you asking fundamental/ core questions about your organization based on a clear mission and stakeholder input– in a way that enhances or adds value to your current operating/business model, mission/vision and goals?

- *Right Problems:* Are you targeting the right problems or challenges that position your organization to lead in its industry, make a difference in society, and be highly profitable?

- *Solutions:* Is the solution based on direction of the core questions and right problems, or is it based mostly on your current mission?

Sample Questions for Assessing Change Readiness

Resistance to organizational change is a negative emotional, mental, and intentional response to a change initiative[25]. Most employees' initial reaction to an organizational change initiative has some degree of ambivalence, where there is a mixture of positive and negative reactions along the three dimensions of emotion, mental, and intention. Allowing the causes behind the ambivalence to be examined and learned from can foster more successful change initiatives by generating new knowledge and new possibilities for understanding and action. Resistance to change that goes unaddressed can cause an organizational change initiative to be delayed, cost more, or fail.

Change Readiness Area	Sample Question
Strategy and Direct Impact	• Do employees understand the project/ initiative goal(s) and change process? • Do employees understand how the change will affect their departments? • Are employees aware of how their jobs will change? • Are employees aware of meetings, training dates and related commitments?

---

[25] Piderit, S. K. (2000), "Rethinking Resistance and Recognizing Ambivalence: A Multidimensional View of Attitudes Toward an Organizational Change", *Academy of Management Review*, Vol. 25 No. 4, pp. 783-794.

Change Readiness Area	Sample Question
Management Processes	• Do employees understand new operating/business processes/procedures they are expected to execute upon implementation? • Are employees capable of performing new processes and procedures?
People	• Do employees understand the task requirements for their jobs? • Do employees have the competencies, skills and abilities to do their jobs to support the change? • What are the best methods to communicate the changes to each department? • Is there a network of employees established to lead and communicate the changes?
Organizational Culture	• How do employees perceive the change benefits for the organization, their department and themselves? • Do employees understand the importance of executing the change as designed • Will performance measures be updated with new performance expectations and/or rewards and consequences based on the change? • Are employees willing to influence/motivate others?

Change Readiness Area	Sample Question
Technology	• Will individuals have access to the technology needed to support the change? • Will the appropriate security changes be made to support the change? • Are there adequate facilities (workspace) to perform effectively?
Organizational Structure	• Have individuals been mapped to new roles? • Have performance measures been updated to reflect new roles and responsibilities? • Do employees understand new reporting relationships? • Do employees understand and support the new organization structure?
Leadership	• Have leaders verbalized support of the change? • Have leaders reviewed the readiness plan and have completed it on time? • Have leaders ensured that constituents schedule and attend training? • Have leaders developed and communicated consequences for non-compliance or rewards for compliance? • Have leaders approved new job mapping/role definitions?

Sample Organizational Change Management Plan

		Timing (Months)											
		1	2	3	4	5	6	7	8	9	10	11	12 ...
1	**Strategy**												
	Realize Need for Change												
	Determine Initiative or Project Purpose												
	Assess Business Case, ROI												
	Approve Initiative or Project												
	Create Strategy- Scope, Goals, Timing												
	Create Tactical Plan- Timing, Activities, Cost												
	Approve Strategy and Tactical Plan												
	Identify Stakeholders												
	Assemble Inititive/Project Team												
	Change Readiness Assessment												
	Assess Communication Needs												
	Assess Training Needs												
	Create Detailed Project Plan												
	Create Communications Campaign/Plan												
	Create Training Plan												
	Create Knowledge Transfer Plan												
2	**Implementation**												
	Gain Leadership Buy-in												
	Manage Stakeholders												
	Manage Risk and Issues												
	Measure Progress, Update Plan												
	Implement Project/Initiative												
	Deliver Communications												
	Deliver Training												
3	**Ongoing**												
	Measure Benefits Realized/ ROI												
	Capture Lessons Learned												
	Update Ongoing Training and Comms												
	Knowledge Transfer												
	Update Ongoing Training and Comms												
	Identify Future Change Needs												

Recommended Resources

Suggested Books/Articles on Organizational Change

1. Kotter, J. P. (2012), *Leading Change,* Harvard Business School Press, Boston.

2. Kotter, J. (1995), "Leading Change: Why Transformation Efforts Fail", *Harvard Business Review,* Vol. 73 No. 2, pp. 59-67.

3. Pink, D. (2011), *Drive: The Surprising Truth About What Motivates Us,* Riverhead Books, New York.

4. Thaler, R. and Sunstein, C. *Nudge: Improving Decisions About Health, Wealth, and Happiness,* Penguin Books, New York.

5. Dannemiller Tyson Associates (2000), *Whole-Scale Change Toolkit,* Berrett-Koehler Publishers, San Francisco.

6. Conner, D. (1993), *Managing At the Speed of Change,* Random House, New York.

7. Burke, W. W. (1982), *Organization development: A Process of Learning and Change (2nd Ed.).* , Little, Brown, and Company, Boston.

8. Gladwell , M. (2000), *The Tipping Point: How Little Things Can Make a Big Difference* Little Brown, New York.

9. Holliday, S. (2012), "5 Ways to Double Your Odds of Inspiring Culture Change", [Electronic Source] Downloaded Sept. 19, 2012 from http://www.greenbiz.com/blog/2012/09/19/how-double-your-companys-chance-success-inspiring-change?page=full

10. Senge, P., Kleiner, A., Roberts, C., Ross, R., Roth, G. and Smith, B. (1999), *The Dance of Change: The Challenge of Sustainabing Momentum in Learning Organizations,* Doubleday, New York.

Suggested Book/Articles on Sustainability

1. Blackburn, W. R. (2007), *The Sustainability Handbook: The Complete Management Guide to Achieving Social, Economic and Environmental Responsibility,* Earthscan, Sterling.

2. Holliday, C., Schmeidheiny, S. and Watts, P. (2002), *Walking the Talk: The Business Case for Sustainable Development,* Berret-Koehler Publishers, San Francisco.

3. Hitchcock, D. and Willard, B. (2008), *The Step-by-Step Guide to Sustainability Planning,* Earthscan, London.

4. Willard, B. (2009), *The Sustainability Champion's Guidebook: How to Transform Your Company,* New Society Publishers, Gabriola Island.

5. Esty, D. and Simmons, P. (2011), *The Green to Gold Business Playbook: How to Implement Sustainability Practices for Bottom-Line Results in Every Business Function,* Wiley, Hoboken.

6. Doppelt, B. (2009), *Leading Change Toward Sustainability, 2nd Revised Edition* Greenleaf Publishing, Sheffield.

7. Sitarz, D. (2008), *Greening Your Business: The Hands-on Guide to Creating a Successful and Sustainable Business,* Earthpress, Carbondale.

8. Macy, J. and Johnstone, C. (2012), *Active Hope: How to Face the Mess We're in without Going Crazy,* New World Library, Novato.

9. Savitz, A. (2013), *Talent, Transformation, and the TBL: How Companies Can Leverage Human Resources to Achieve Sustainable Growth,* Jossey-Bass, San Francisco.

10. Elkington, J. (1998), *Cannibals with Forks: the Triple Bottom Line of 21st Century Business,* New Society Publishers, Gabriola Island.

About Scot Holliday, Ed.D.

I am the Founder & President of Change Tactics. My expertise is in organizational change management, sustainability, climate change, and energy. I serve as a change leader, advisor and researcher; depending on the need at hand. I typically work on a project-basis directly with companies, trade associations, government and not-for-profit organizations. I work independently with clients or jointly with other firms to provide broader services to clients, e.g. East Meets West Solutions, LLC. Previously I served as a Senior Organizational Change consultant, both at IBM and Accenture.

Contact info: see webform at www.changetacticsllc.com/contact.html

About Change Tactics

Change Tactics works directly with organizations to create successful change. Our unique approach is utilizing the power of people that currently exists inside an organization. Solving a problem requires more than simply identifying the solution, it involves implementation and results delivery. Throughout the process of working with a client we apply organizational change management— the process of leading people through a planned change process. When change is planned the likelihood of success is twice as likely as unplanned change. Our product is not simply a report; it is an organization that performs better. For more information see our site www.changetacticsllc.com

Our Mission

The mission of Change Tactics is to increase our customer's business success through problem solving and organizational change management in a way that has a positive benefit to society and the environment.

The Value We Deliver

- Increasing human performance
- Deliver better services and products to customers
- Achieving your business performance goals
- Being more aware of emerging trends for your business— seeing current blindspots and foresight into what is on the horizon
- Doubling the chance of successful change

Our Philosophy

All organizations must deliver results in order to survive. People are motivated when their particular knowledge, skills and capabilities contribute to success. Great organizations appeal to customers, employees and other stakeholders. To be great, people have to perform well, operations must be effective, and the services & products delivered must fulfill one or many needs of the customer. In addition, throughout the development and delivery of services and products, it must be executed in a way that has a positive impact on society and the environment.

Our Services

The foundation of Change Tactics is leading organization change. We tailor solutions to meet customer needs. In creating a solution some of the areas we draw from are as follows:

- **Problem Solving**- Our approach to problem solving is based on examining core questions, diverse stakeholder input and clarifying the mission at hand. Based on this foundation the right problems can be identified, leading to the right solutions.

- **Strategic Planning**- Sharpening an existing business strategy, integrating social and environmental considerations into your strategy, gap identification or creating an entirely new strategy.

- **Process Innovation**- Increasing the efficiency and effectiveness of management or business processes. This may include human performance, energy efficiency, water efficiency, reducing materiality, and making services or products more sustainable.

- **Employee Engagement**- Make employees active participants in change. Communicate and train employees how to make your business a success. Create performance measures and goals that drive desired actions.

- **Organizational Alignment**- Aligning the people within your organization to a new or existing strategy. This includes identifying barriers and ways to overcome them for each department or business area.

- **Organizational Transformation**- Plan and implement change throughout the organization using all the relevant levers for organizational change management

Notes:

Notes:

www.ingramcontent.com/pod-product-compliance
Lightning Source LLC
Chambersburg PA
CBHW050522210326
41520CB00012B/2403